Let's Move : Dot Marker Adventures With Wheels & Rides

by Happy Kids Press

FORKLIFT

TRAILER

SEGWAY

AIRPLANE

MOTORBOAT

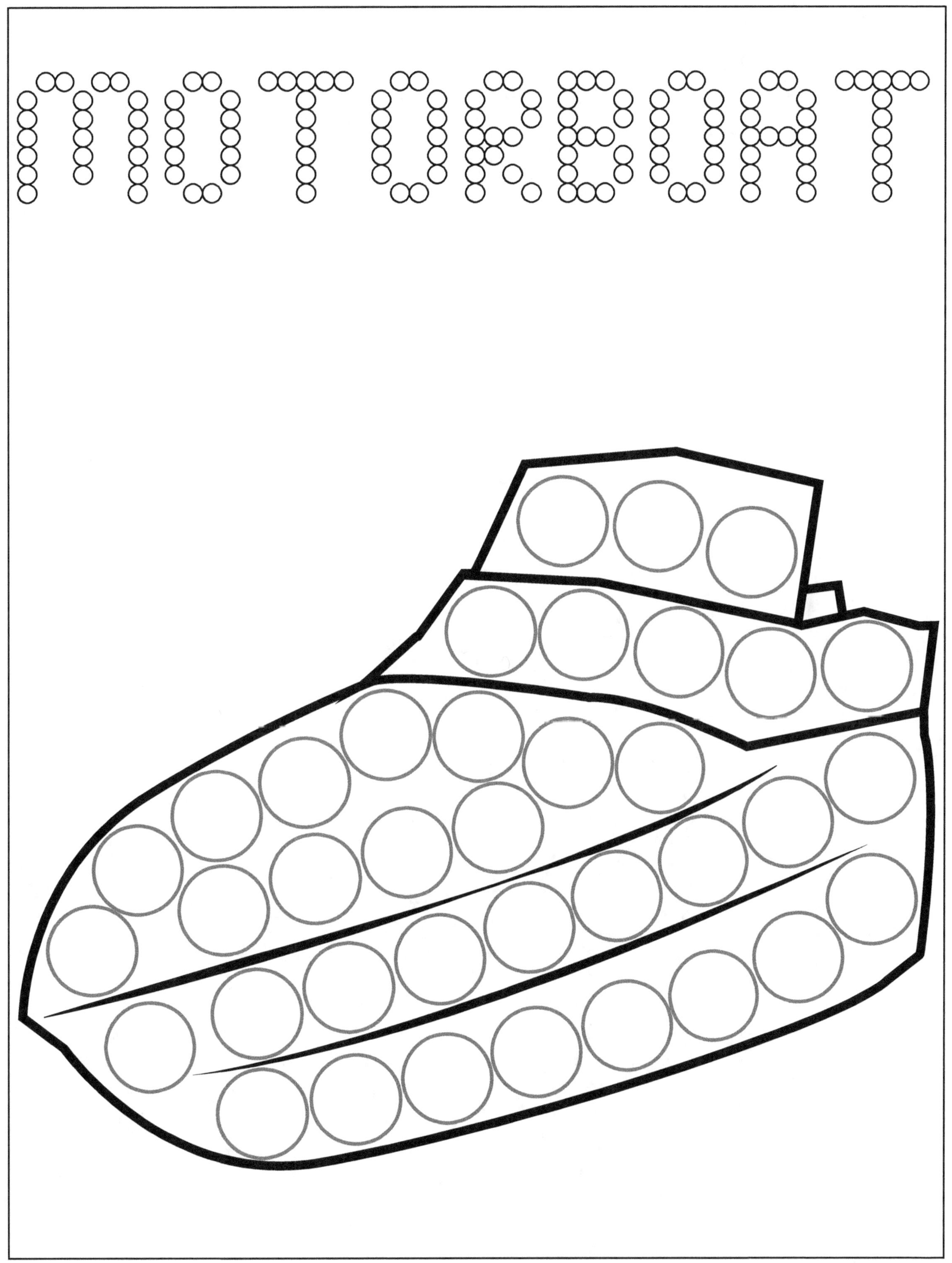

CONCRETE MIXER TRUCK

ROLLER SKATES

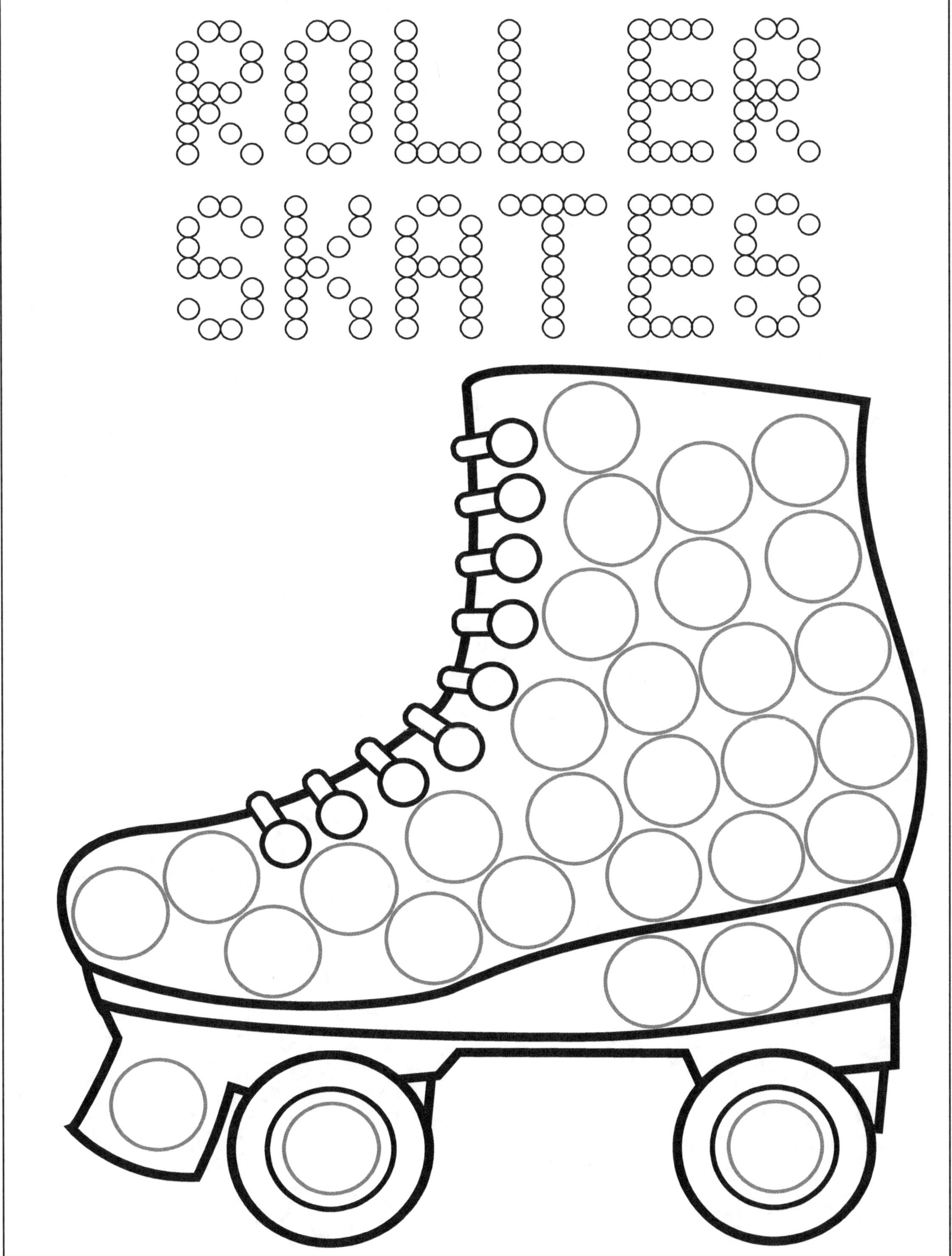

TRACTOR

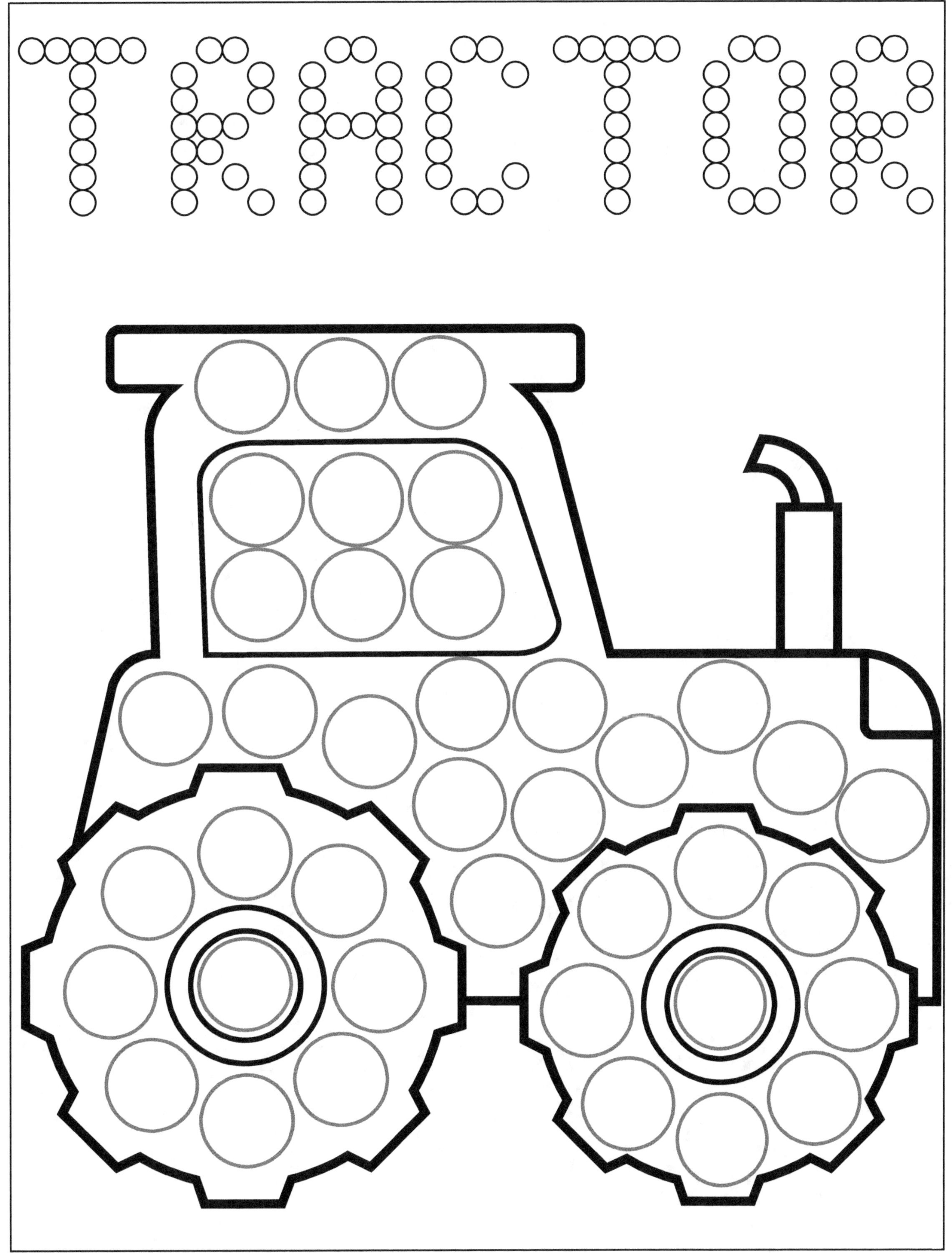

DUNE BUGGY

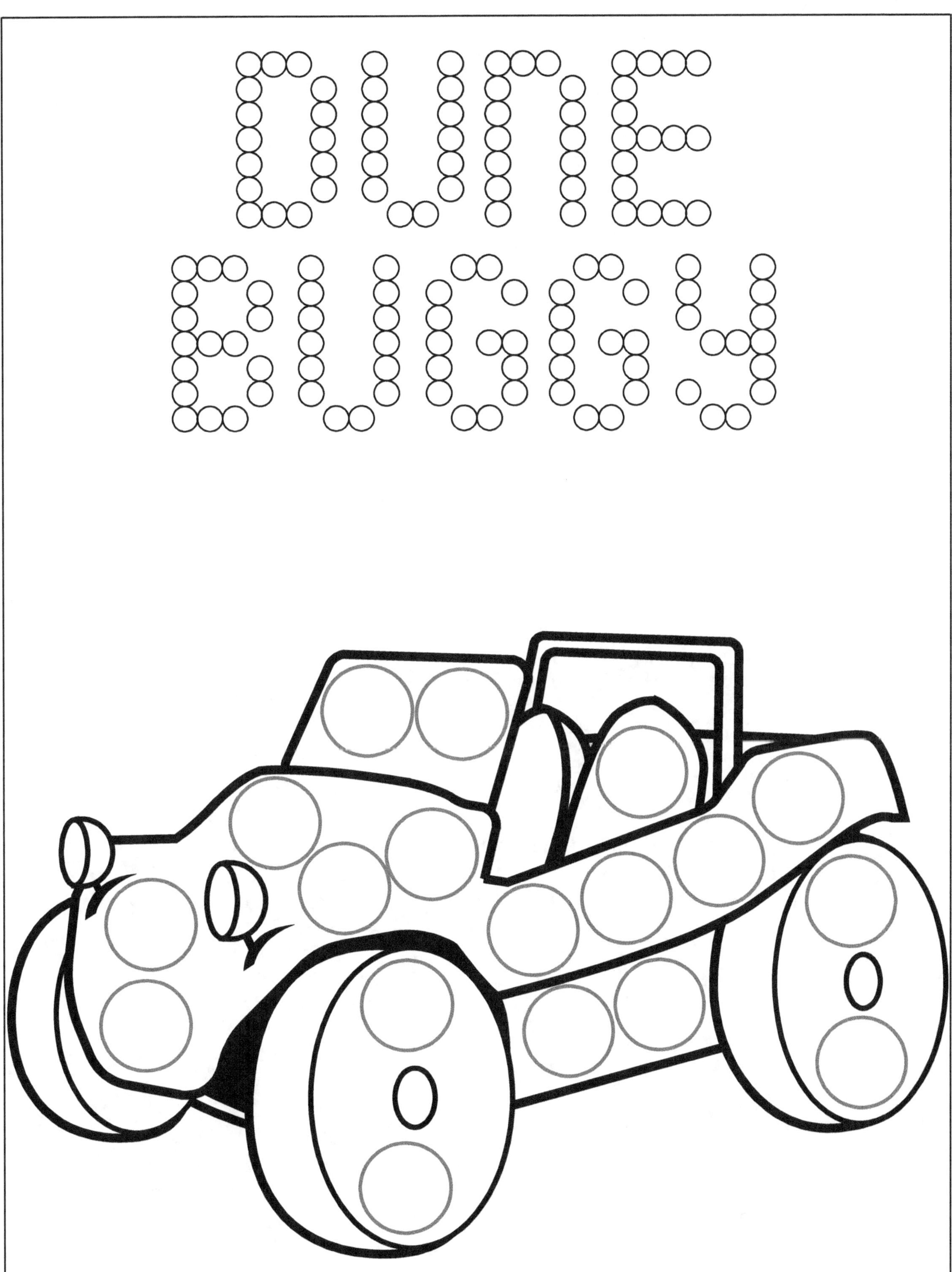

TANKER
TRUCK

Limousine

SKATEBOARD

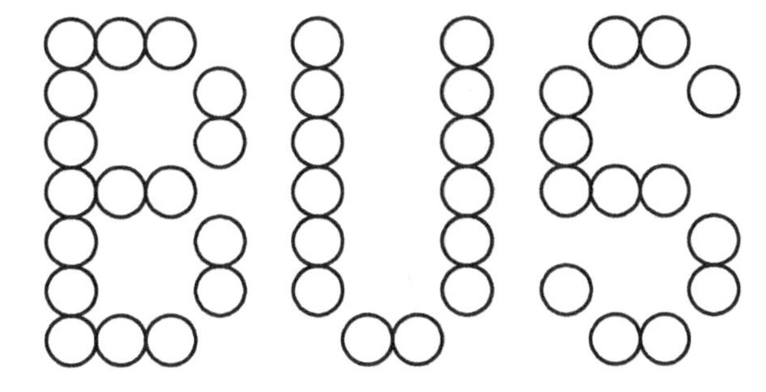

ATV

TOW TRUCK

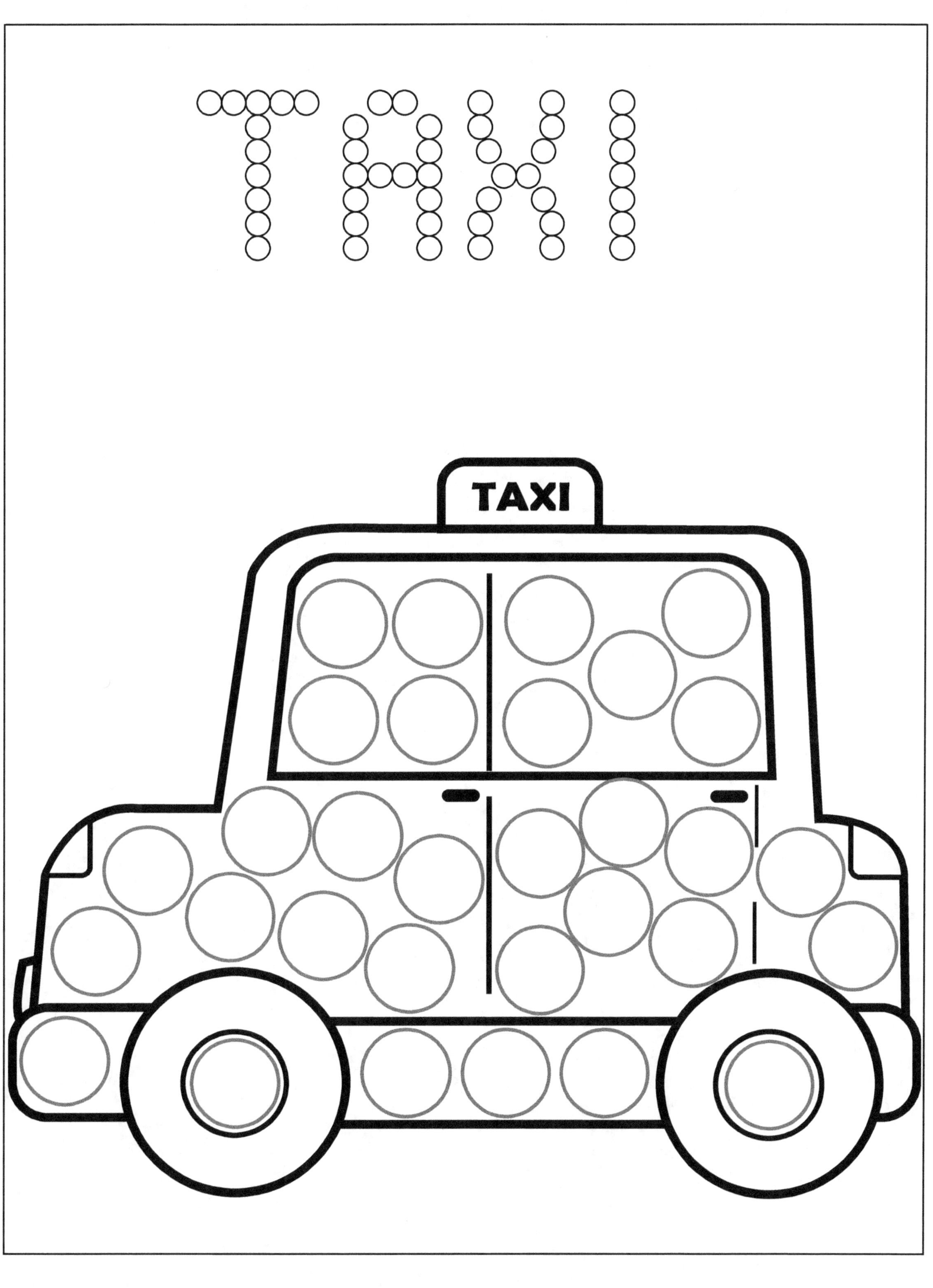
TAXI
TAXI

SCOOTER

BICYCLE

PARAGLIDER

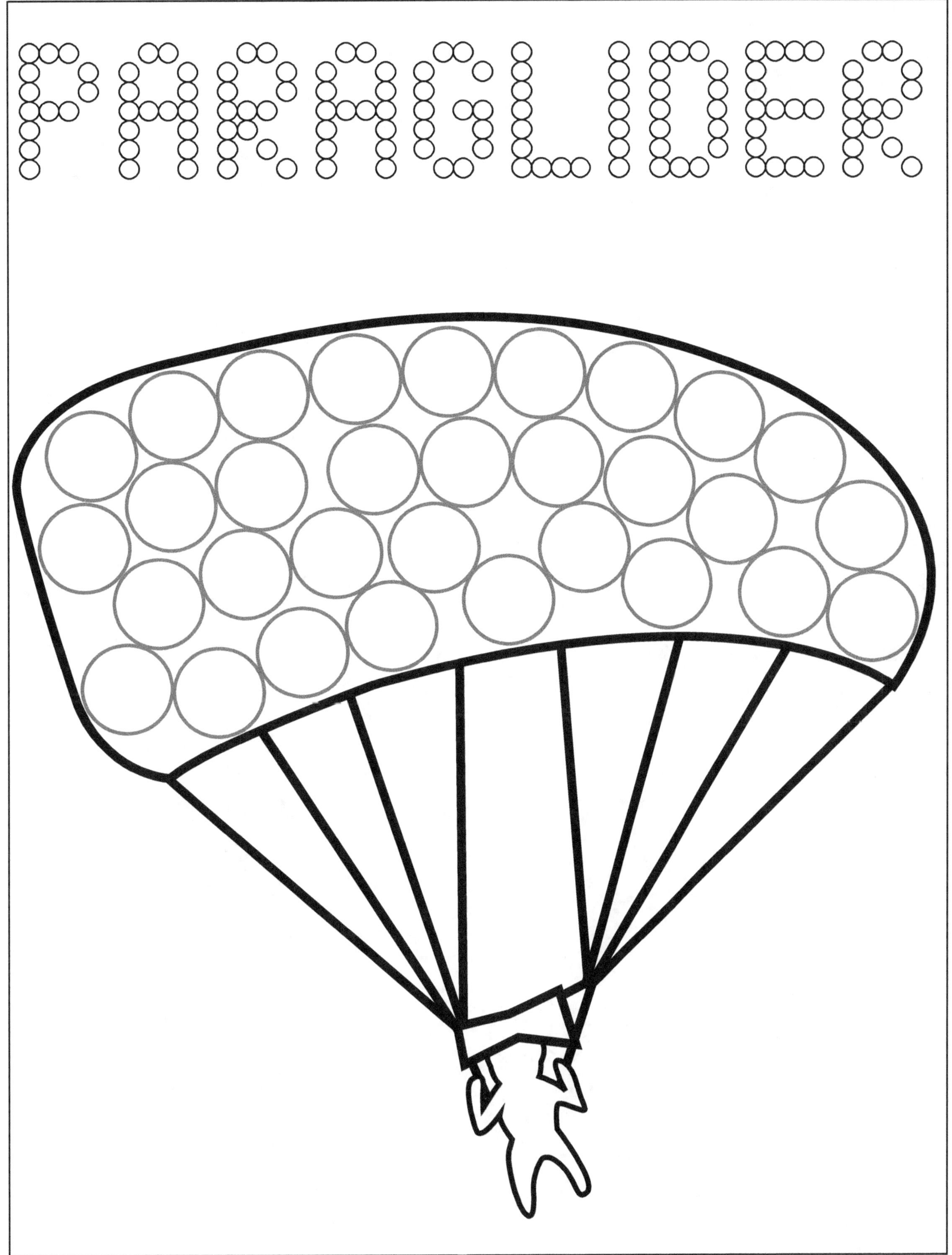

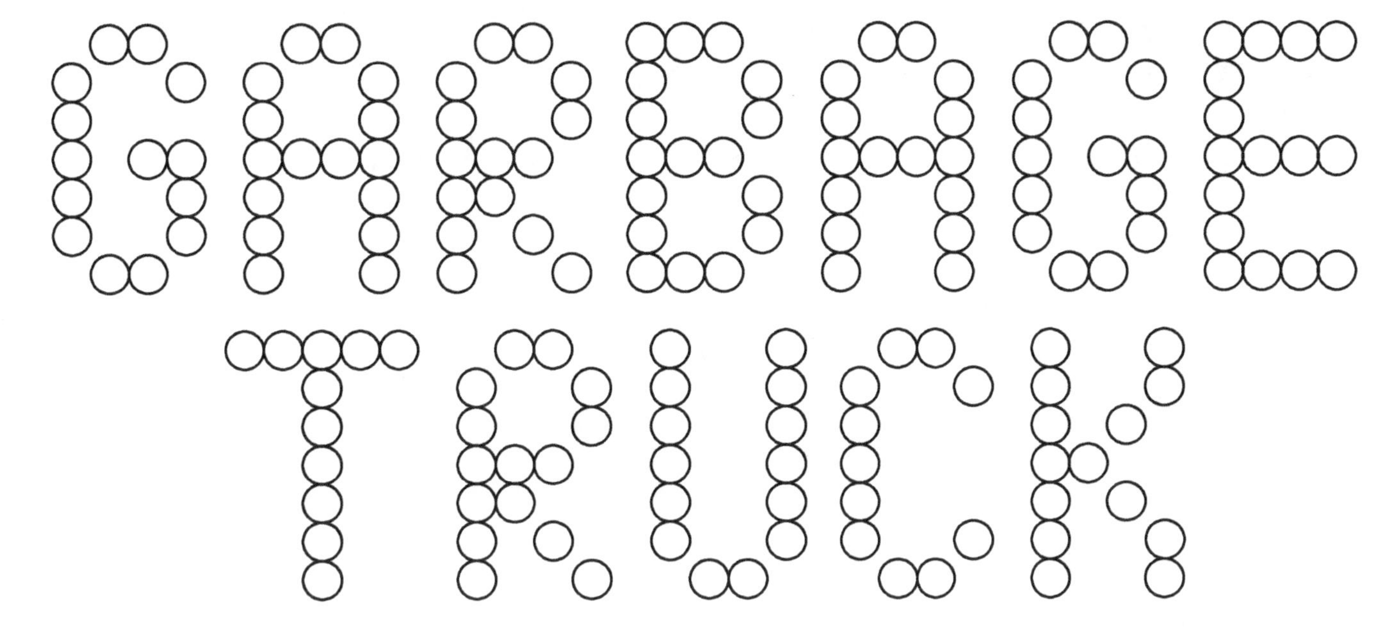
GARBAGE
TRUCK

POLICE CAR

YACHT

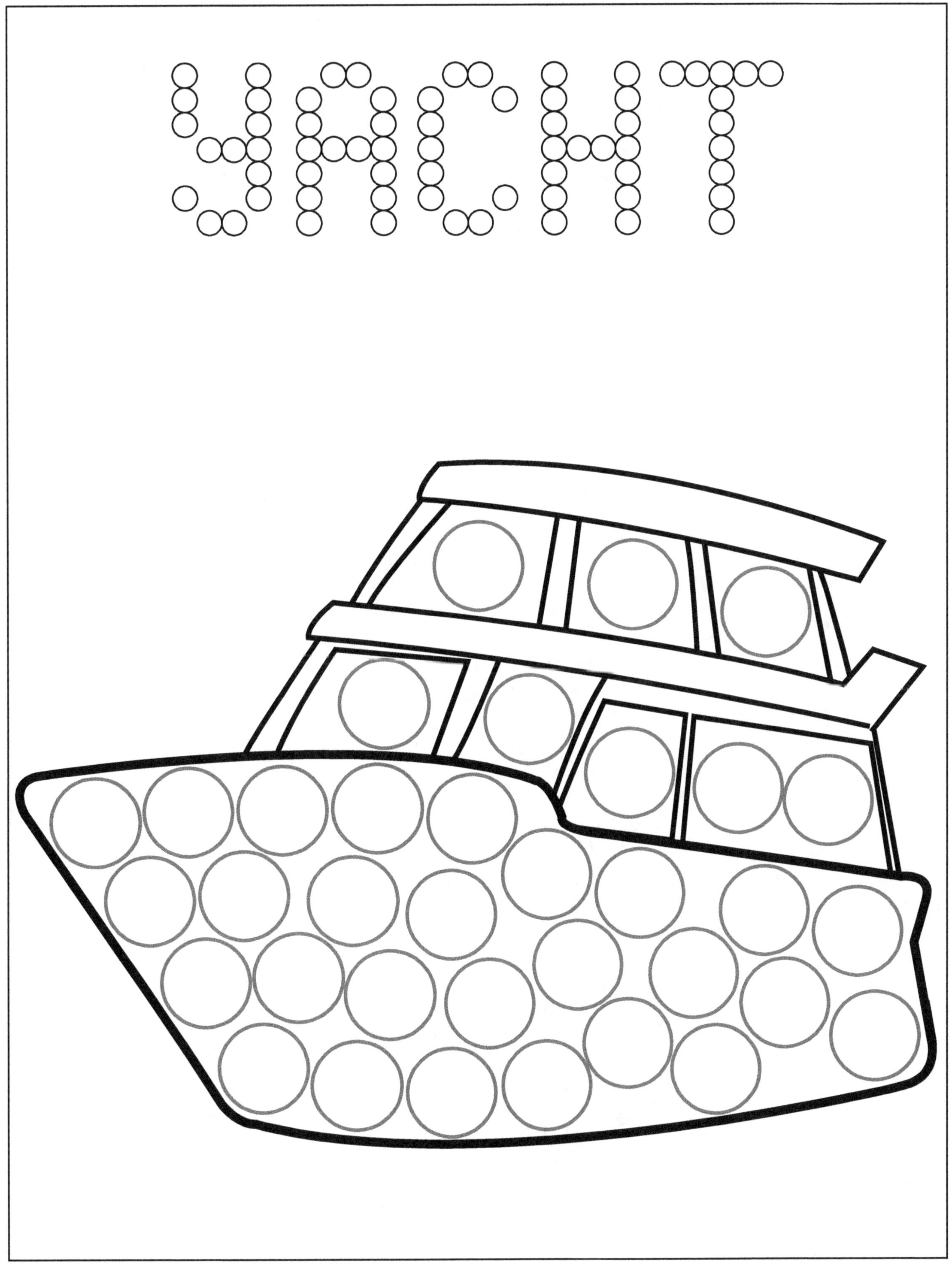

MOTORCYCLE

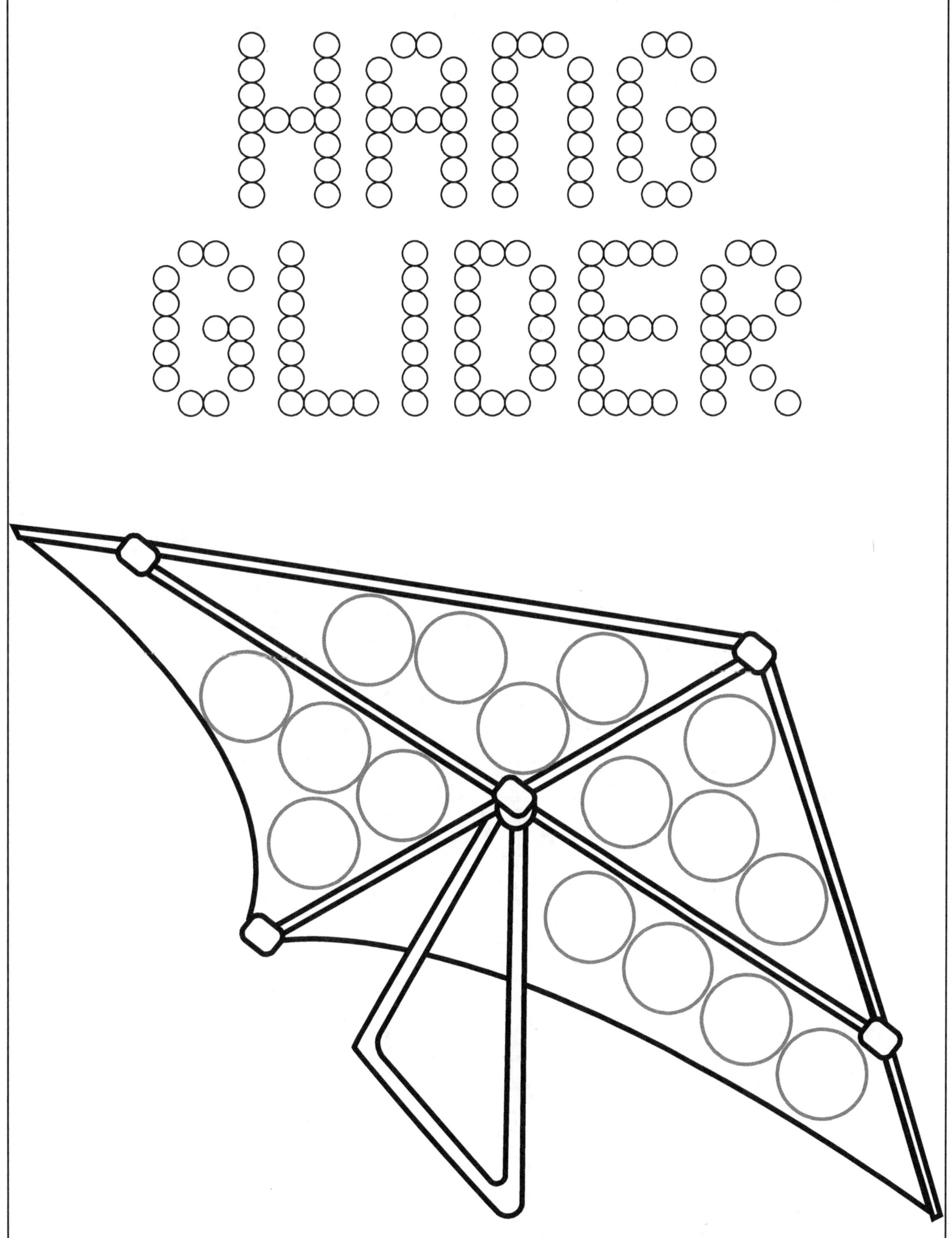

HANG
GLIDER

DUMP TRUCK

FIRE TRUCK

JET SKI

Van

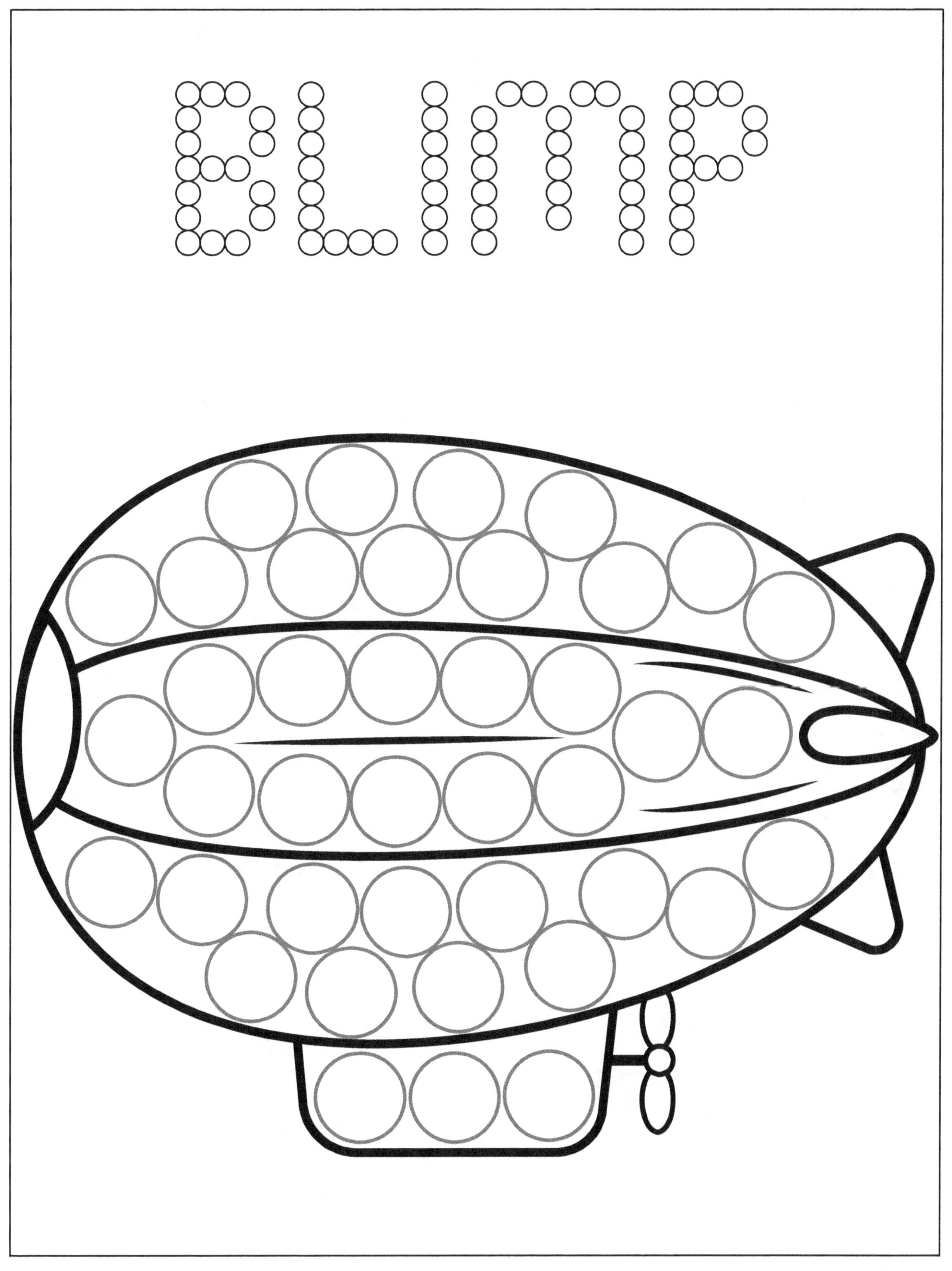
BLIMP

EXCAVATOR

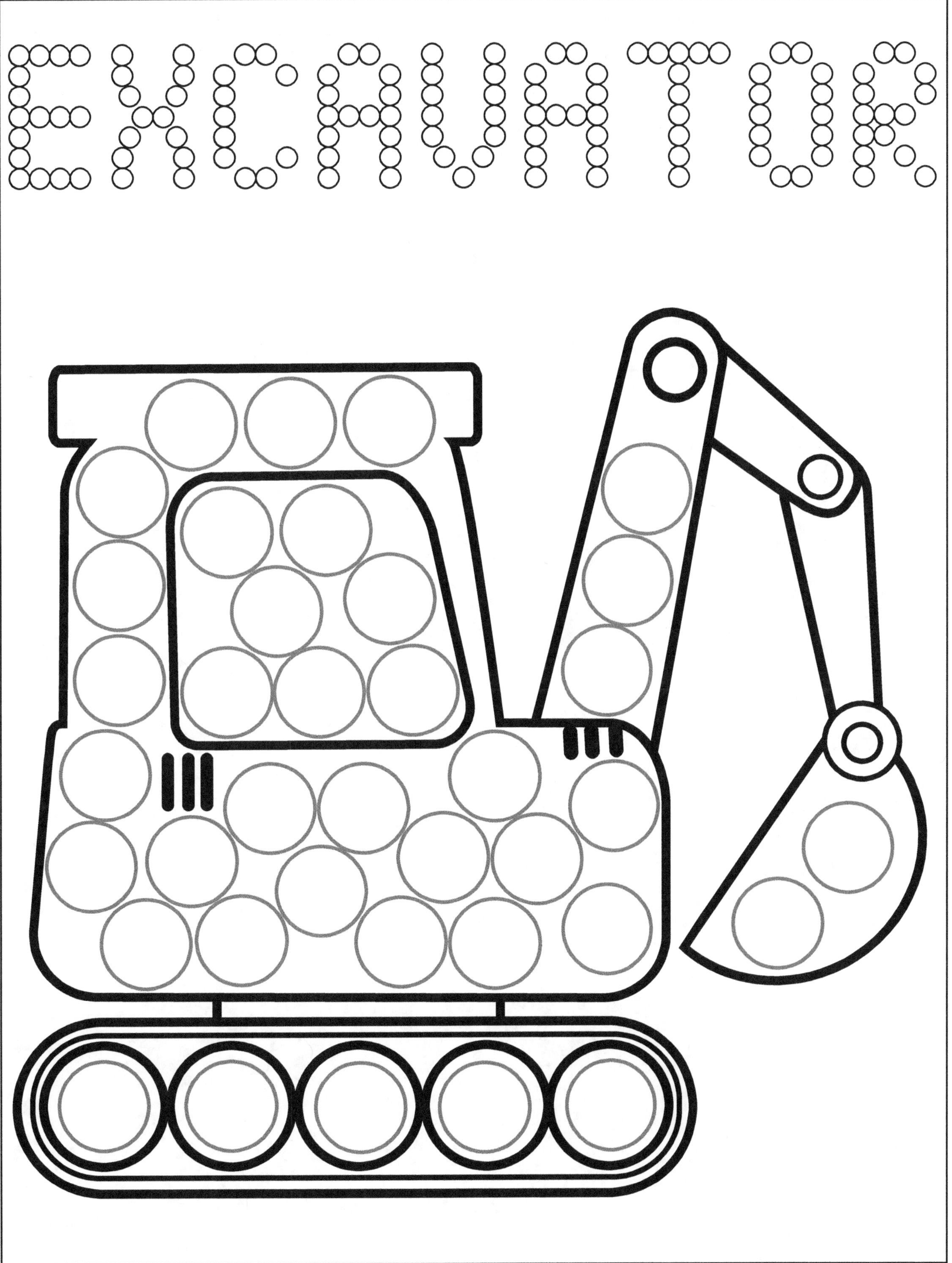

AMBULANCE

BOAT

SUV

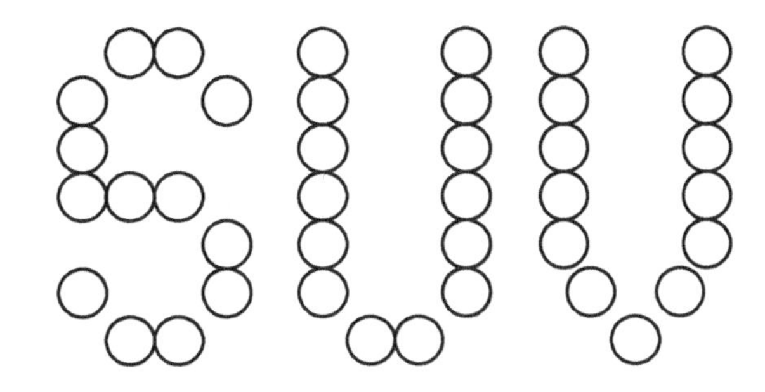

HOT AIR BALLOON

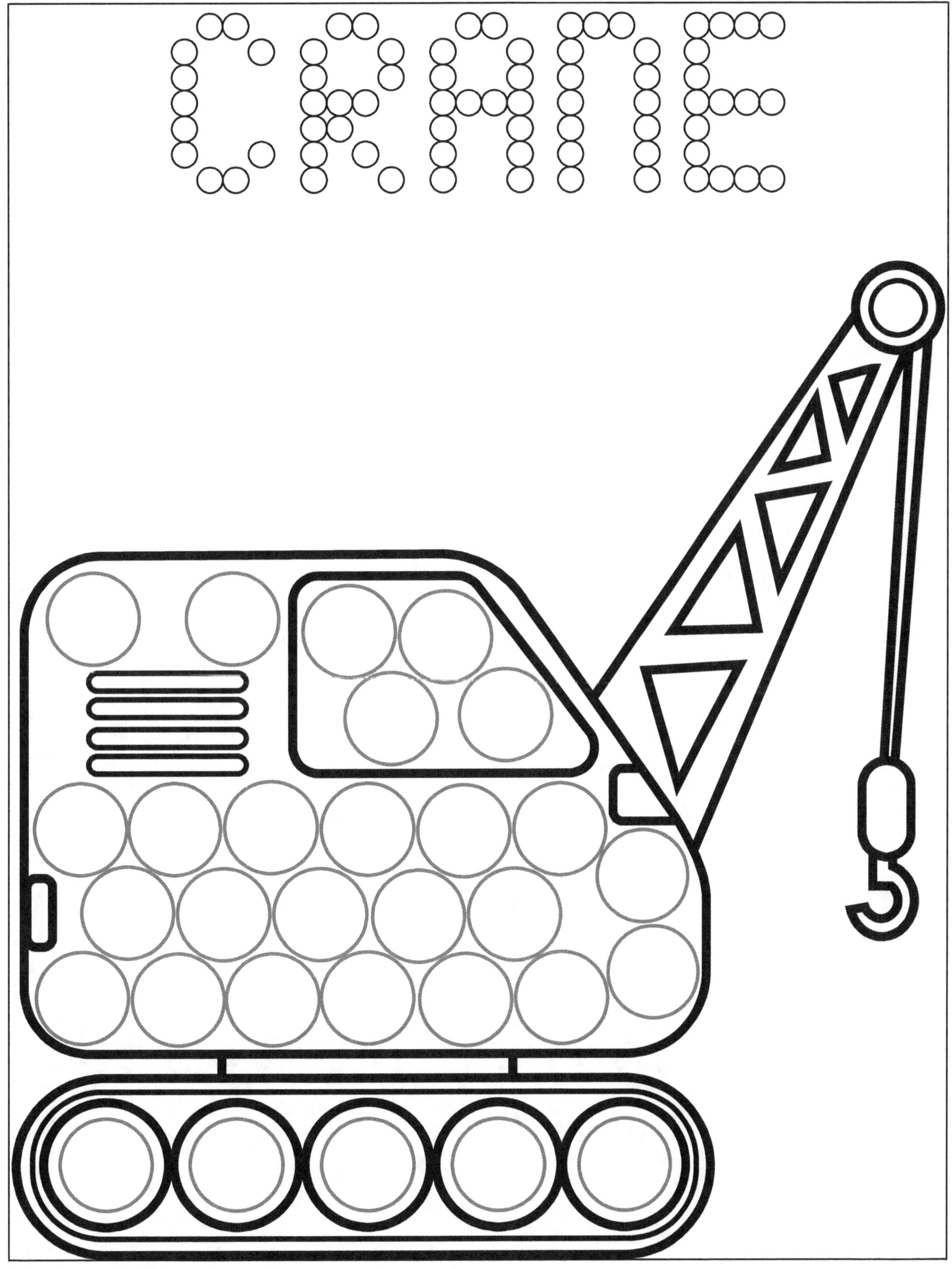

CRANE

GOLF CART

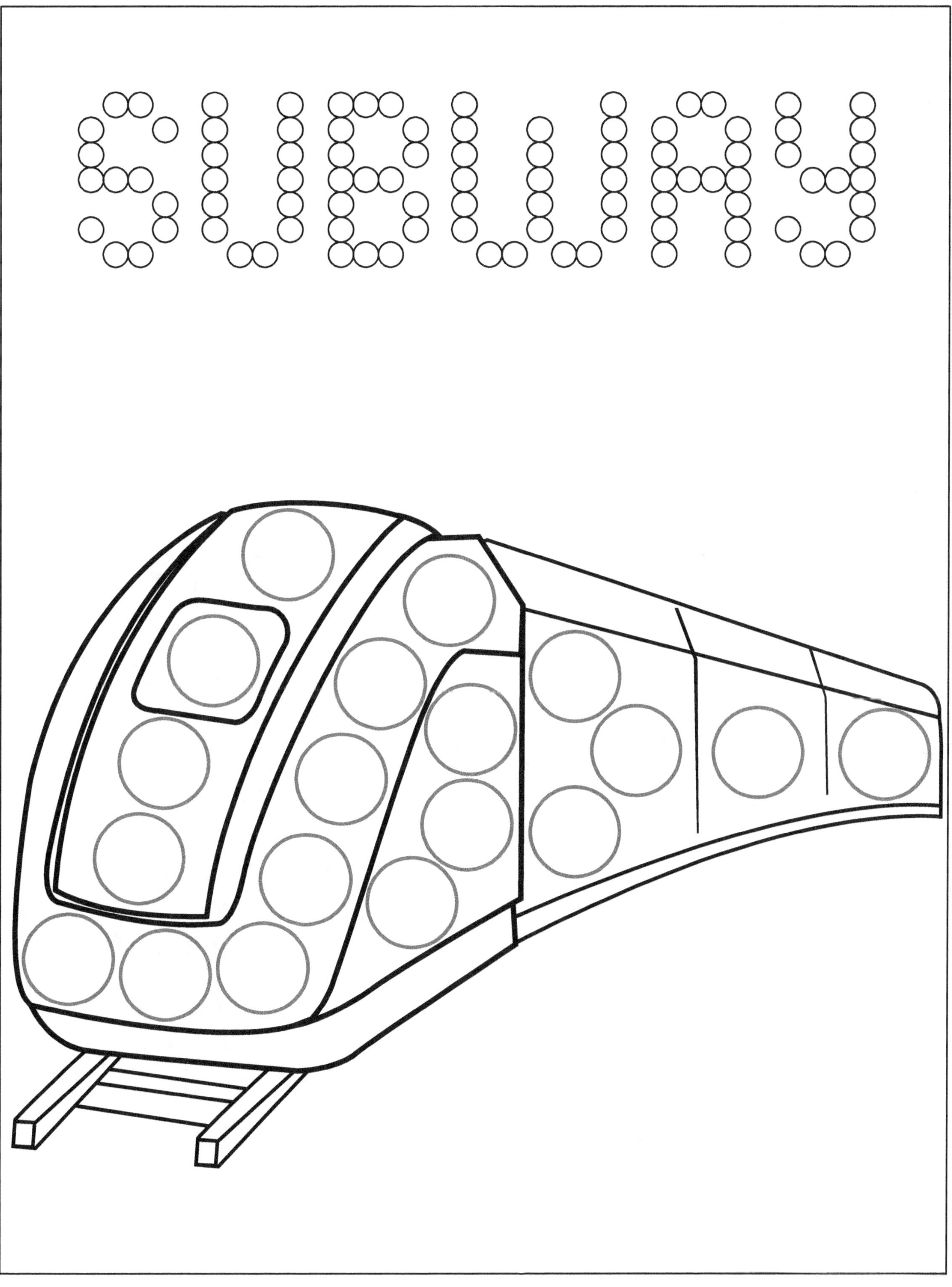

SUBWAY

TRUCK

TRICYCLE

BULLDOZER

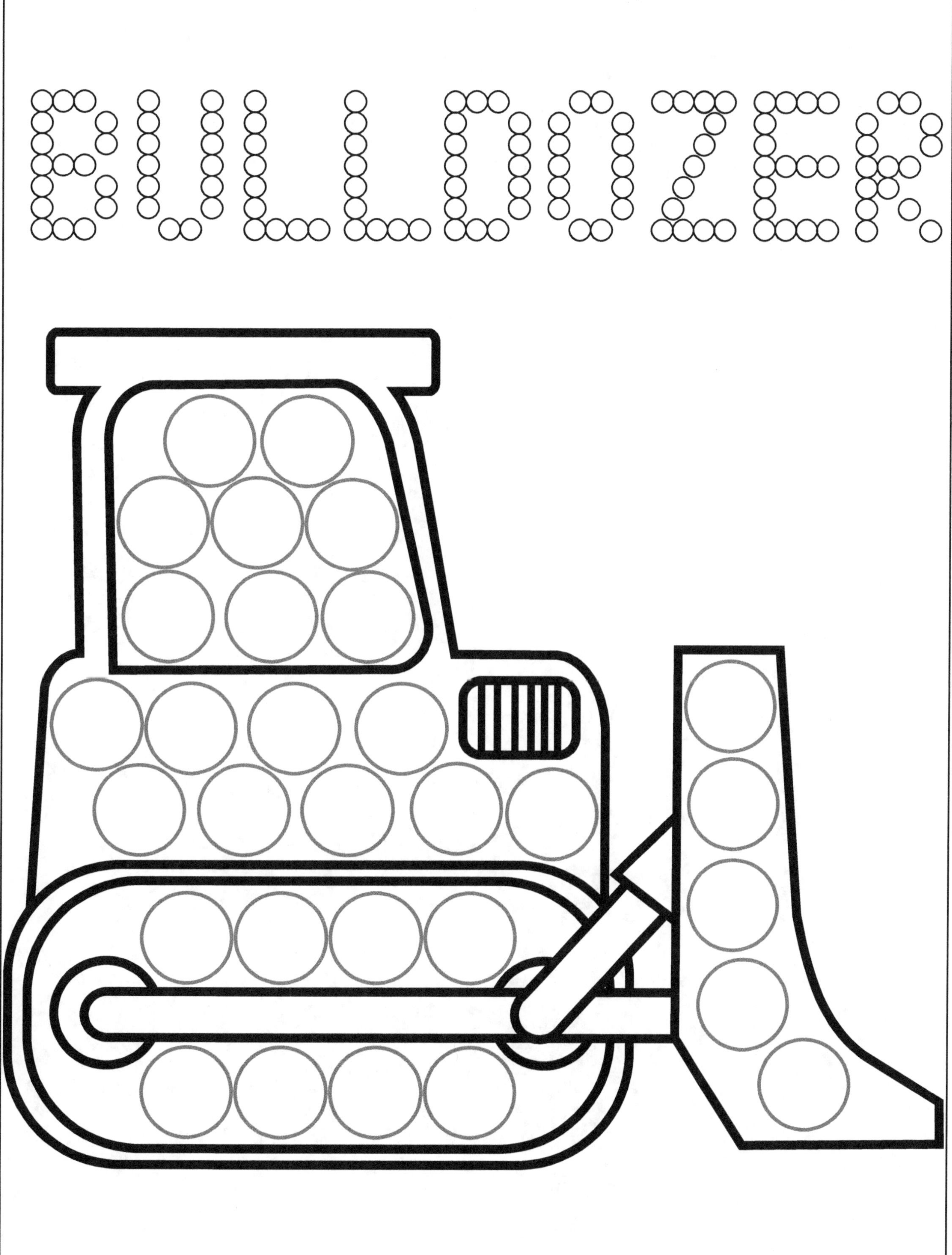

snowmobile

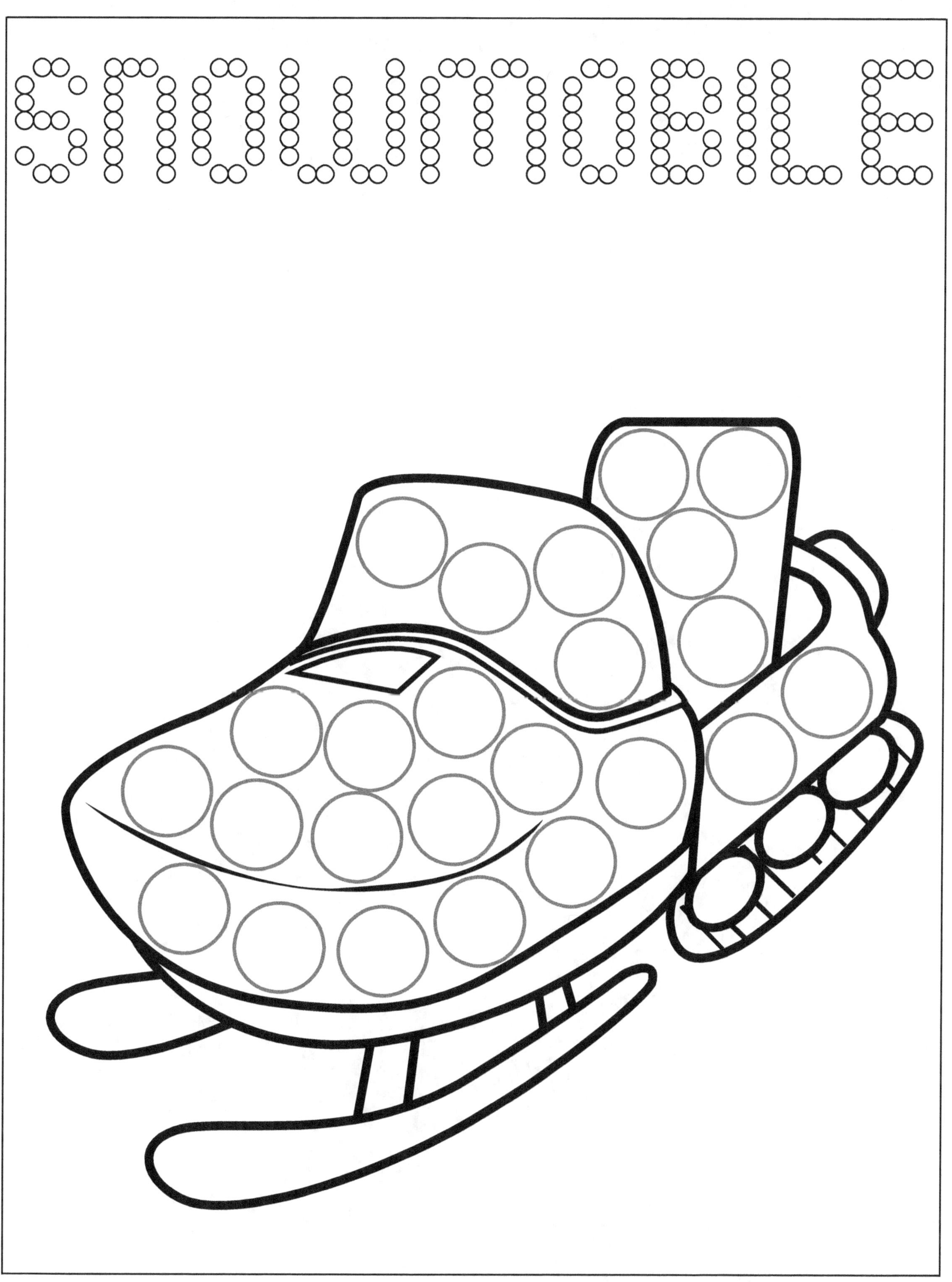

TRAIN

CAR

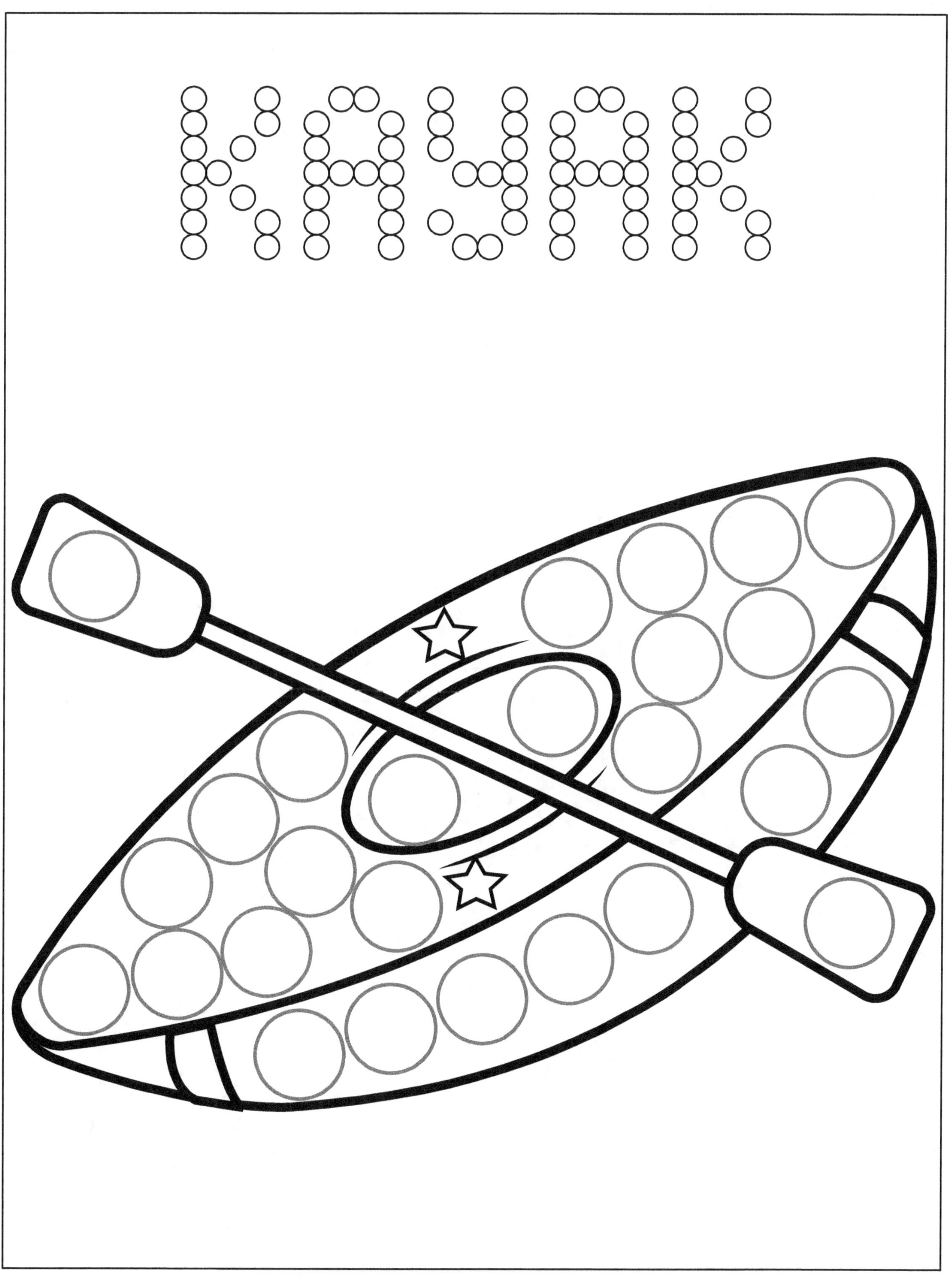

KAYAK

LAWN
MOWER

CAMPER

ELECTRIC BIKE

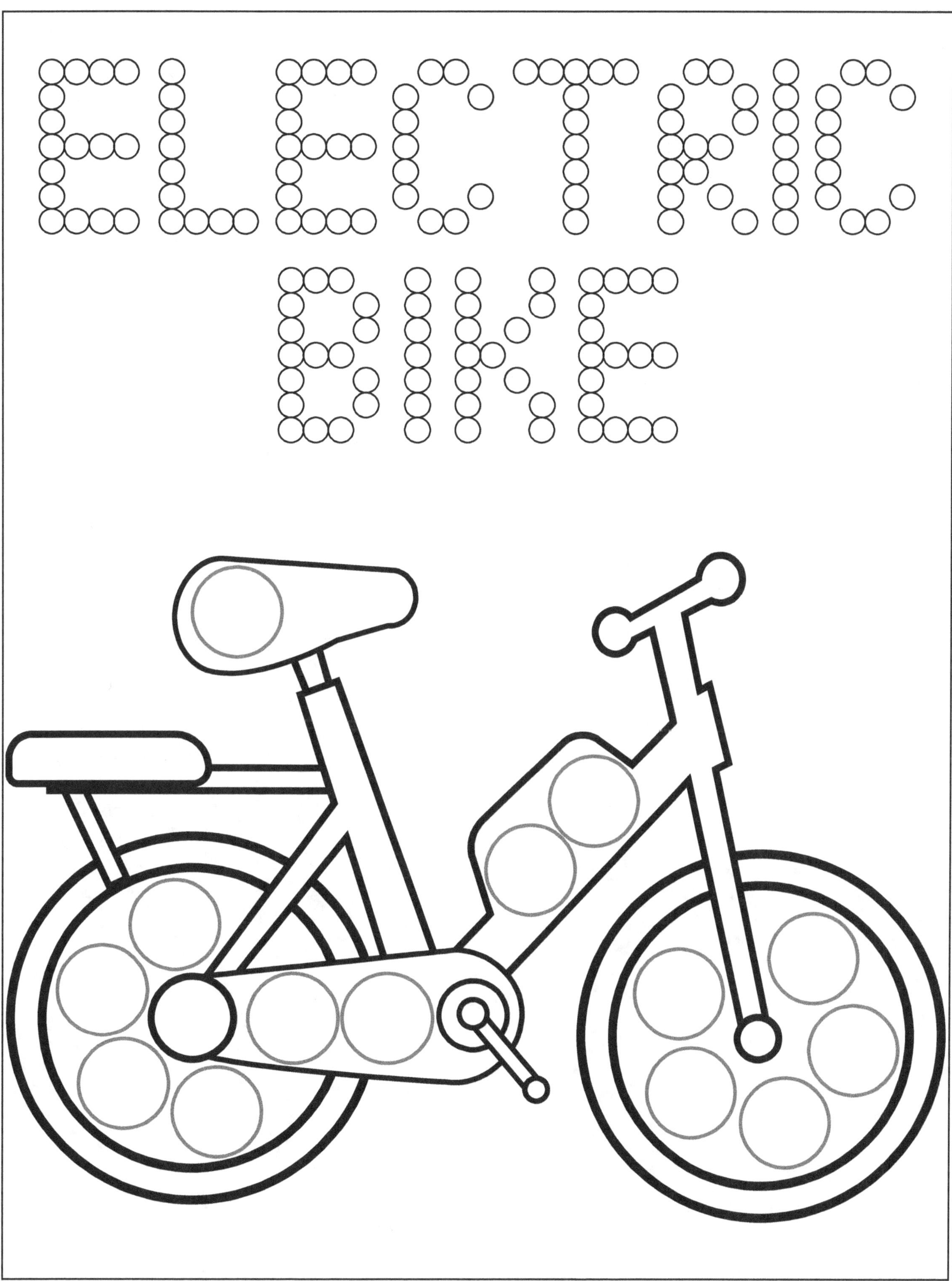

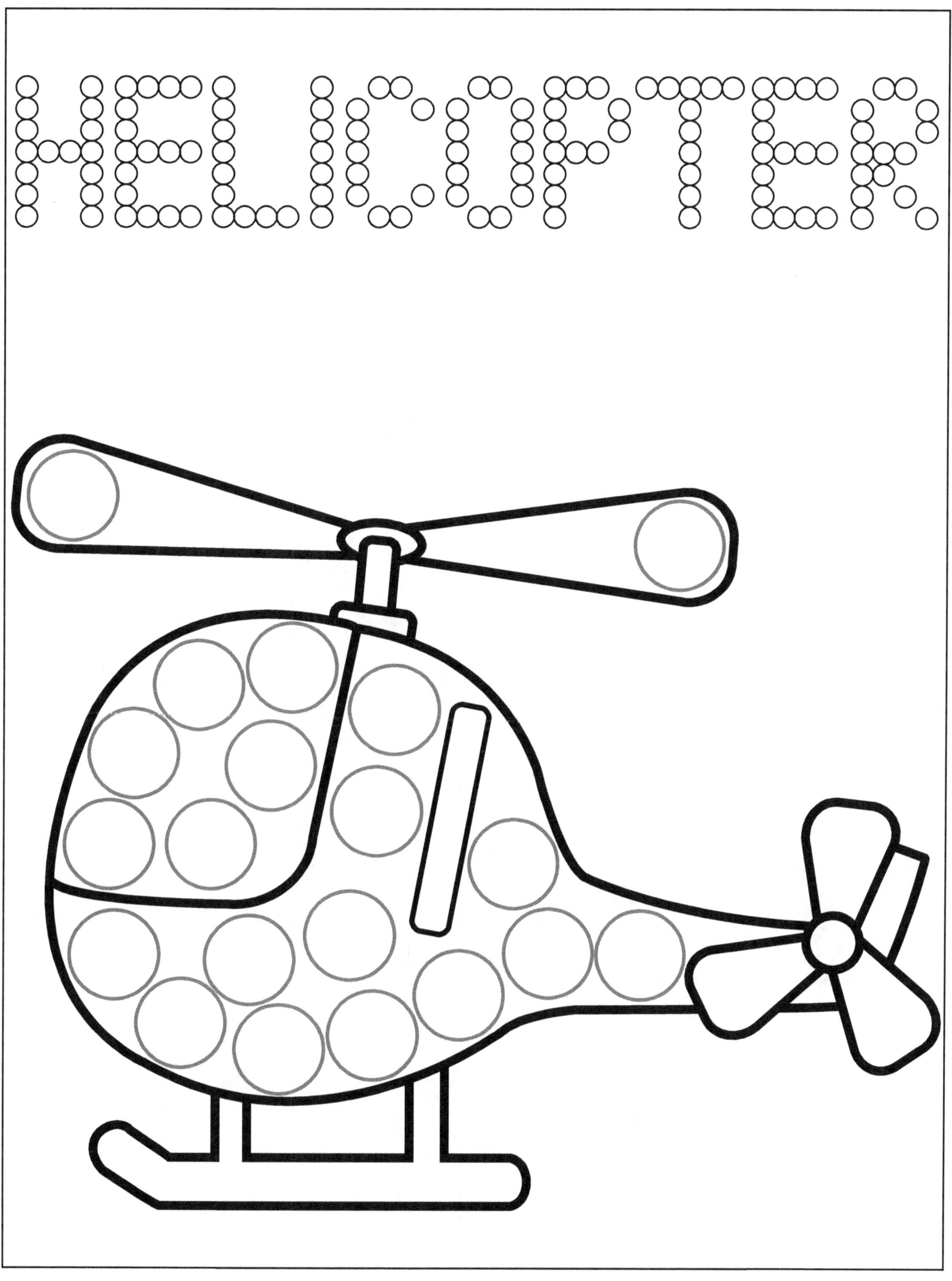

HELICOPTER